Just a Farm-Raised Canuck

By
Rose Aline Russo

PublishAmerica
Baltimore

© 2009 by Rose Aline Russo.
All rights reserved. No part of this book may be reproduced, stored in a retrieval system or transmitted in any form or by any means without the prior written permission of the publishers, except by a reviewer who may quote brief passages in a review to be printed in a newspaper, magazine or journal.

First printing

PublishAmerica has allowed this work to remain exactly as the author intended, verbatim, without editorial input.

ISBN: 1-60703-834-X
PUBLISHED BY PUBLISHAMERICA, LLLP
www.publishamerica.com
Baltimore

Printed in the United States of America

Dedication

This book is dedicated to my siblings Lorraine & Oswald Bourque, Laurida O'Brien, Jeannette Patriquin, Bertrand Belliveau, my children Pam & Carl Russo, Debra & Abel Picard, Gary Russo, grandchildren Austin & Nevin Picard and especially my husband Salvatore Russo.

Acknowledgments

I owe thanks to my husband Salvatore Russo who kept supporting me throughout and helped in every way possible.

I also owe thanks to my daughter Debra Picard for her secretarial skills in helping me with formatting and correct punctuation.

Author's Note

Looking back on my life I realize the blessings of being born and raised in a quiet country setting with the values being the love of family and neighbors. The little village I came from was all related and ready to help if needed. Those values have allowed me to be very happy with the little things in life as opposed to needing numerous material goods I treasure the fact that my husband and I am in good health and able to share a good movie and dinner together. Life today seems so stressed and harried that I thought it might be interesting to compare, leading me to write my memories down. I hope everybody will find my book interesting and amusing.

Just a Farm-Raised Canuck

Chapter 1

Hi! I am Rose Aline and I was born in Memramcook, New Brunswick, Canada. I am the daughter of Alyre Belliveau and Exeline (Brun) Belliveau. I am the fourth daughter out of six siblings. My three older sisters, Lorraine, Laurida and Jeannette plus two younger brothers Dollard and Bertrand complete the family. We lived on a farm on Little Dover Road in Memramcook, New Brunswick, Canada. My memories growing up there are all very positive. My Mom and Dad were fantastic parents. They were very warm and every one of us grew up as individuals. We were a very close family and had very few arguments. They were very much in charge and I do not ever remember any of us getting slapped. They just had a way about them that made you want to be good.

My dad was a very hard worker on the farm. Due to the way

things were in those days, he was pulled out of school in the second grade to work the farm. Therefore, he never learned to read and write. Dad always felt bad about that so he was very stern about us never missing school without a real good reason. Despite that handicap he was very smart with money and every day business. We had a large garden that gave us all fresh produce so vegetables were plentiful. We had two work horses named Kitt and Belle to plow the land and we also had cows for milk and butter which we churned ourselves.

We had chickens which gave us our eggs. He would fatten a calf and a pig yearly for our beef and pork meats. When he slaughtered the calf and pig, he would bring it to the butcher where different cuts would be made giving us roasts, steak and hamburgers which were kept in storage. Some of the pork we salted in barrels down the basement to be used in boiled dinners etc. So our food was provided for but what we did not have is money. Any bills such as taxes and other things that required money meant he had to go on his wooded land and cut some pulp or firewood to be sold for cash so he could pay his bills. Sometimes he would get lucky and get some work pouring cement foundations for contractors. That always made him happy and he really felt good getting a paycheck. He was always sad when it came to an end

Dad never learned how to drive therefore we did not own a

car so visiting relatives was limited. They basically had to come to us since most of them had cars. A visit from anybody was a real treat.

Harvest time and hay time were always difficult for dad since he had four daughters first and the boys were too young to help. It is really difficult to do a load of hay or oats alone so when I was thirteen or fourteen and being a tomboy that preferred outside work, I started helping him do the hay. He would pitch the hay up and I would make the load. It may sound like a simple thing to do, but it is not. You have to place the hay around the wagon so it goes up even or else it gets too heavy on one side making the load lopsided causing the load to tumble on the way to the barn. That is a mess take my word for it. I learned the hard way. But after a while I was a pro at it. Also, the cows had to be milked everyday so if he had to be away for any reason we had to milk the cows. I really did not like that.

Chapter 2

It is not easy to describe my mom. She had the patience of a saint. She never complained about anything and she always had a smile on her face. My fondest memories are remembering that smile that always made me feel safe and loved. It was not uncommon to hear her hum through the house as she did her housework.

I never remember her snapping at me no matter how tired she must have been at times. She worked very hard in those days. She made her own bread. Monday was laundry day which was always a disaster. We would have clothes all over the place. Laundry meant scrubbing on a wash board one piece at a time, rinsing and then passing through a ringer to get the excess water out. and then hung out to dry on the pulley line. You always wished you had a nice windy day so it would dry fast so you could refill the line often. It was always an entire day affair.

Cooking meant going in the garden to pick what you were going to cook first. Mom also sewed most of our clothes. She was real good at sewing. It was actually more like tailoring. We were always the best dressed because she would receive barrels of clothes from dad's brother's family from the USA. She would unsew these garments and turn the material inside out and sew us some outfits including dresses, coats and snowsuits. All it would cost her was labor and thread. She made her own patterns with brown paper bags and would use the catalogs to see the latest styles and copy it.

Then in Canada they had a family allowance which was a check by the government that provided a certain amount of money for each child. She would take that check to Moncton (the city) and buy us footwear and items that she was not able to make and budget the money on a twelve month basis and just turn over the check each month. So actually, it was a charge account. She did all the painting and wallpapering around the house and always kept the house nice.

Chapter 3

I would like to elaborate farther on my siblings. There are some oddities in my family for obvious reasons. My two older sisters were born not even a year apart but then mom lost four babies after that. It was the RH factor and in those days they did not know how to save the babies. Because of that, there is twelve years difference between my oldest sister and me. Therefore, when I was four years old, my sister Lorraine was sixteen years old and working in the city of Moncton. And when I turned five years old my sister Laurida also went to work in Moncton. They had a room together there and only came home on weekends. That was a big help to my parents as they could now dress themselves and help mom and dad financially at times. Jeannette is ten years behind Laurida and I am two years behind Jeannette. Dollard is four years behind me and Bertrand is a change of life baby and ten years behind Dollard. So as you can see, we are a three step family. It makes the two oldest closer to each other and the four youngest closer together.

Chapter 4

The eight room house we grew in had four bedrooms upstairs, kitchen, dining room, living room and a large family room downstairs. It was heated by the wood burning kitchen stove and a wood burning belly stove in the family room. There was no heat upstairs, just tons of heavy blankets on the beds. The bathroom was an outhouse outside so believe me you made sure to make a bathroom stop before you went to bed because getting up in the middle of the night and going outside was not an option in the cold winter. Nobody lingered there because of the cold so you did not wait on anybody.

In the summer the flies and smell would rush you up. I was twelve years old before we got electricity in 1950. Before that everything was done with kerosene lamps. There was no TV. We had a little radio that ran on batteries on which we listened to one French soap opera called "Seraphin". We use to listen to Ford Theatre. The shadow knows and to Wheeling West Virginia on Saturday nights and also the French Montreal Canadians (hockey). We had to make the batteries last so we could not play it all day.

We also had a manual crank gramophone on which we played 33 1/3 RPM records. Lorraine and Laurida bought the records in Moncton. I remember hearing Ernest Tubbs and Hank Snow a lot. I guess they were favorites of my sisters. There were no telephones at that time. Ironing meant heating the irons on the wood stove because of no electricity.

We had spring water piped down from my grandfathers springs located at the top of his property. He had three or four different springs there. He also had a large open tank filled with water and people could fill up buckets if they were short of water. We were fortunate enough to have a cousin that was a plumber so we had the water piped in the kitchen stove so we had hot water without heating up water on the stove. That was a luxury that the other neighbors did not have.

You have not lived until you get a Saturday night bath in an aluminum tub in my time. First you carried the tub upstairs then you carried buckets of hot water to fill the tub up. Then you worked on getting your body into that little tub and scrubbed with some home made soap that just about took your skin off. But you felt like a million getting your once a week scrubbing. Then of course you had to haul all the water back down in buckets and get rid of it. Showers work much better let me tell you.

Chapter 5

My favorite spot was the verandah going around two sides of the house which contained two swings. My brother Dollard and I would swing on them for hours and sing. We learned to harmonize pretty good with "Ashes of love" and "As long as I live". But mostly that was our favorite pastime. Then eventually, the verandahs were knocked down and a front porch was added, but I always preferred the verandahs. The house was located on acres of farm land. The land belonged to my paternal grandfather, Simon Belliveau and passed on to his son. The house was moved there from another location. That house holds many happy memories. It is where all the younger generations would gather and just shoot the breeze and feast on mom's delicious home made fudge. Life was good. Night entertainment growing up was a card game between Jeannette and I and Dollard and Dad after our homework was finished. We played until 9:00 p.m. then went to bed.

Chapter 6

The seasons when I was growing up in Canada were very different than now. The summers were beautiful. It would climb to the mid eighties or the beginning nineties but it was dry and not much humidity, so the sun would feel good. The nights would cool right off and you might even need a light blanket making it nice sleeping weather. The air was very clean and free of pollution being in the country with no factories or manufacturing around. I also remember beautiful rainbows after it rained.

The winters were harsh and long. We would start wearing fur lined boots in October for warmth and would stop wearing them in May when the mud dried up. The snow would come up to the window sills on the house by January. It would drift all around the house so high that we used to dig tunnels and play inside. Also the snow was drifted so hard that we could walk on it and we would not sink. I remember at least two winters where the snow plow could not open the road because the snow was too deep and hard and the plow kept breaking. Cars were unable to use the road so the only way to travel was with a horse and sleigh or on skis and snowshoes. Now that I think about it we were very lucky that nobody ever got seriously ill. Then finally it would be spring and guess what we had a dirt road no pavement so you guessed it, mud with all the melting snow. So the road was not passable until May when the mud would dry. Some years were a little easier when they could keep the road open. We had mud and deep ruts but the cars could get through. The roads are now paved and they have street signs which are a big improvement. The winters are a lot less severe.

Chapter 7

School was a one room school house that taught grade one through eight. It had a big pot belly stove in the middle for heat and desks all around it. One teacher taught all the grades. It was two miles from our house so we walked four miles a day to go to school. There were no school busses. We went to school for 9:00 am and got home at 4:00 PM. When they could not plow the roads, we went to school on skis. All the children in the village did winter sports such as skiing, ice skating and tobogganing so we were all good on skis. School in Canada is dual language so we learned French and English for the entire twelve grades. In order to better master both languages, we would speak French in the morning and English in the afternoon in school. The teacher would ignore you if you were not using the correct language at the specified time.

When I was entering into the seventh grade an agreement was reached with Father Masse and the Pre D'en Haut High School that the seventh grade through the twelfth would go to that school. Pre D'en Haut had some school busses so we would be bussed there. This was good for everybody since the bus had to go by the little school house. The bus gave them a ride to the little school, so there was no more walking for them.

My high school years I was taught by nuns and I am here to say that they are the best teachers ever. They analyze each student potential and insist that you meet that potential. If they feel you are an A student, which I was, they push you to accomplish it. By the same token if you are a C student they expect at least a C. They really cared for all their students and gave all the help they could to help you achieve.

I loved school and I did not want to be absent ever. I even missed school during the summer. I was involved in school plays which were beautifully directed by Sister Gaetane. I loved acting in those plays. I learned my lines right away. It was fun.

I went to the High School until the tenth grade and then I moved to the United States with my family. I would eventually finish my high school at night in the USA and receive my High School Diploma.

Chapter 8

Little Dover Road was like a village. There were 9 houses and everybody was related. Up the top of the hill was William Belliveau at the bottom of the hill was Max Belliveau, (Dad's two brothers and my uncles). Across the road was Addia Cormier and down the road was Phylias Cormier (two brothers) and dad's cousins. Across from Phylias was Tilmon Cormier and down below Emile Cormier (two brothers) across the way was Clovie Le Blanc and Antoine Cormier. Antoine Cormier was Grandma's brother therefore Dad's uncle. Clovie LeBlanc was married to Antoine Cormier's daughter. So that is how the village was all related.

The unity of the village at times was exemplary such as when the firewood for the winter needed to be cut to size. They would have somebody with a saw come to the village. All the men would get together at one house and work on cutting the wood and then move on to the next house until the whole village's wood would be cut. No money changed hands, they would just exchange time. Whatever house it fell on for lunch, the wife would cook the meal for all the guys and the next house would cook dinner. I loved the smell of sawdust throughout the whole village and also the friendliest joking and laughter amongst the men. Each house would split their own wood and stack it in the wood shed for the winter.

When we had a bad hurricane and our barn was knocked down, all the guys got together and in one day the barn was back up. They were always there for each other when there was a tragedy. They would come and volunteer. You never had to ask.

Chapter 9

Our house was located right below Uncle Max's house. I used to really love Uncle Max because he was such fun to be with. He was always pleasant and singing funny little songs to make us laugh. My dad was more quiet and serious. But Uncle Max was more entertaining. He also had a model T car and used to let us ride on the back bumper holding on to the big back tire. Dad used to frown on that safety wise but we loved it. He had three children cousins, Paul, Edgar and Therese. I always loved my cousin Paul. We used to play so well together whenever my Aunt Anita would let us play together. I do not know to this day why she would not let us play together at times even when Paul used to cry and beg her to let us. Paul and I used to like to run away from Grandpa. Grandpa was very grumpy and would watch everything we did and somehow would find something wrong all the time. So we would crawl under the fence and he could not get us. I do not get to see my cousins much, but they do cross my mind often and they all turned out very special as far as I am concerned.

Chapter 10

My Uncle Willie lived on top of the hill above Uncle Max's house. He was great too and when we grew older he would give us transportation to Moncton on the way to work and bring us back home after work. No busses ran from our area to Moncton back then and Moncton was twelve miles away. My cousins Della, Annette and Terry were younger so we never really hung around much although we are pretty close to Della. My Aunt Zella is real nice too.

Chapter 11

My sister Lorraine married Oswald Bourque in 1946. I was eight years old at that time. Wedding receptions back then were held in the homes. I remember all the festivities being done the week precluding the wedding. All the women of the village gathered at our house to make fancy sandwiches and to bake a bunch of pastries. They would chatter and exchange pleasantries as they accomplished these feats. It was fun and exciting for me to watch all this and I would get caught up in the moment

Lorraine and Oswald bought a house in Dieppe. We still had them visiting us with their daughter Wanda. Then in 1953 after taking their papers out, they moved to the USA. Now we were really missing all of them. Dad was missing them the worst because both his sons-in law were helping him here and there.

They were carpenters and they would provide the labor and dad the materials to fix different things needed on the house. They were also male companions to interact with. They both had a lot of respect for dad and liked him a lot so dad missed talking and laughing with them.

Lorraine and Oswald would go on to have six children, Wanda, David, Judith, Oswald Jr., Claude, and Phyllis.

Chapter 12

My sister Laurida was married to Tilmon O'Brien in 1948. I was ten years old. The same preparations were done. When I was 11/12 years old, I used to love to play tricks on everybody and he had such a good sense of humor about it. He would play tricks on me too in return and we were always teasing each other and laughing

For a period of time, Laurida and Tilmon lived with us. Carpenter work was not that plentiful then so Tilmon would have to work away and only come home on weekends. This was lousy for both of them.

In 1952, after taking out their papers, they moved to the USA. We missed them terribly. Knowing it was a better life for them we adjusted and life went on. They came home in the summers for a week or two and we enjoyed that.

Laurida and Tilmon would eventually have five children, Claudine, Kenneth, Paul, Daniel and Timmy. Years later, my sister Laurida and her husband Tilmon moved back to Canada. They built a house on an acre of family land near the family homestead.

In the year 1995, we lost Laurida's husband, Tilmon and my brother-in-law whom I was very close to. Tim as we called him was sadly missed by everybody. May he rest in peace. Laurida still lives there today.

Chapter 13

Now to lighten up on all these statistics I would like to share some amusing moments hopefully to give you a few laughs.

One of my task as I was growing up was to collect the eggs in the chicken coop. One morning as I was doing just that, I noticed this hen who had just laid an egg and I wanted that egg now. Well, the hen thought differently. She was not ready to give this egg out yet. I reached under her to get the egg and made her angry so she pecked at my hand. Well, I was not happy so when she got off the nest, I followed her outside and picked up a little metal bar and hit the chicken on the head. The chicken started to stagger all over the yard and my Dad coming from the barn saw her. I quietly went into the house, washed my hands and sat down for breakfast. Dad said I don't know why but one of my chickens does not look so good. I did not say a word and he did not push. It was years later when I was grown up that I told him but I think he always knew and let me get away with it.

We had this little pig that my dad was fattening up for the kill later on and this little pig did not want to stay in the pen. No matter what we did, he would dig under and get out and we would have to chase after it trying to catch it. I do not know if any of you have ever tried to catch a pig, but let me tell you it is difficult. The three of us were running after it full blast and just when we would reach out to pick it up it would change direction on a dime and we would still be running but in the wrong direction.

Mom was in the dining room at the window watching us and she was laughing so hard, tears were running down her face. We would eventually catch it but we sure got our exercise out of it. We would also be laughing our heads off because that little pig was so cute that we could not be mad at it.

I mentioned earlier how deep the snow would get. One day I got a bright idea so I thought. I grabbed the toboggan and climbed up to the top of the roof on the shed. I put the toboggan down, got in it and went sliding off the roof. That was bad enough in itself but down the bottom was a barb wire fence. I did manage to duck and make it through but in the process scared the living life out of mom who immediately grounded me. I was such a tomboy I tried everything.

One time Oswald and I decided to go trout fishing. We did not own a pole so we would just cut a vine and tie a string with a hook and a worm. Then you would dangle the worm under a rock in the brook and a lot of times you would catch a trout. That particular day we were not having any luck. We fished for a while and we finally decided to quit and go home. When we got home, a whole bunch of company had come. I was about thirteen or fourteen years old and I was extremely bashful and sensitive. When we walked in somebody asked did you catch anything? Without thinking of what I was saying, I blurted out "the fish ate all of Oswald's worms and we could not catch it. At that, the entire room roared with laughter. I realized what I had said and ran to my room embarrassed and crying.

There were many Sundays spent with the O'Briens. My brother-in law Tilmon came from a family of eighteen siblings. His Dad drove a truck that resembled the truck driven by The Beverly Hillbillies on the television program. Picture that truck with all the kids in the back. It was a different sight. We were so happy to see them come because we had a lot of children to play with. The grown ups would play bridge (a card game) so fun would be had by all.

Then there was my brother Bertrand that was one of our

pastimes because when he was two, Dollard was twelve, I was sixteen and Jeannette was eighteen so everything Bertrand did was funny to us. We spoiled him something awful. Bertrand was very independent and he had a temper only because we teased him all the time. He would get mad at us and open the door in the cold winter to get even. We would use reverse psychology and say, "Oh Bertrand, how did you know we were too warm? That is great, leave it open". He would slam it shut because he did not want to please us. He was so cute. We loved him.

Another time he was going outside and I happen to be behind him and saw the baby skunk walking along. All of a sudden Bertrand goes, "oh a pussy cat" and he takes off to catch the skunk. I am behind him running and trying to catch him before he reaches the skunk. I just barely made it and grabbed him and ran like heck the other way. We were lucky not to get sprayed. So there was never a dull moment.

One time, Mom sent him to wake me up. He definitely woke me up. He hit me over the head with a heavy glass coke bottle! I woke up all disoriented and not knowing where I was for a minute or so. I never knew why but I guess I must have deserved it.

One time Lorraine and Laurida were learning to drive with a small delivery van that said "Mom's Doughnuts". Well

Laurida was a pretty good driver but Lorraine forget it, she was always silly. She would begin to laugh and forget what she was doing and Laurida was serious and yelling at her to put the brakes on. Like idiots we were going for a ride. We were so excited going for a ride we never considered the danger. But they were funny driving that little van.

Youngest son Gary with nephews
Nevin and Austin Picard

Eldest son Carl and his wife Pamela Russo

Our daughter Debra and her husband Abel Picard

Eldest Grandson Austin Picard

Grandson Nevin Picard

Sister Laurida and her husband Tilmon O'Brien

By Beloved Parents
Exeline and Alyre Belliveau

Brother Dollard and Rose Aline

Homestead as today

Original homestead look

Sister Lorraine and her husband Oswald Bourque

Rose Aline and her husband Sal Russo

School house attended on Little Dover Road

St. Thomas Church in St. Joseph which I attended

Exeline and Alyre Belliveau's childen
Jeannette, Rose Aline, Bertrand, Lorraine, and Laurida

Chapter 14

The memories of meal time stick in my mind. We would all eat together and that is when we would share the happenings of the day. What we did at school good or bad or what was troubling us and helping to solve each other's problems. We would linger for as long as it took before cleaning and washing the dishes. These were always happy times with lots of kidding and laughter.

The meals in Canada consisted of a lot of boiled dinners such as green beans cooked with pork in a pot along with boiled potatoes and cabbage or potatoes and carrots boiled in a pot with pork. We do have some special dishes though. The famous one is "poutine rappe". The ingredients are: grated potatoes, cooked potatoes and cut out pieces of pork in the middle. You mix both potatoes together and form into a ball.

Poke a little hole in the middle and add the pork, cover, roll in flour and drop it into a pot of boiling water. We also have "Rappe" which consist of grated potatoes and watered down bread with added oil and butter and baked in the oven until crispy. We did also have meals of steak and roast. A lot of vegetable soups made with all the fresh vegetables from the garden.

Chapter 15

I was a pretty good softball player. That was another of my youth enjoyments. I enjoyed my friendship with my girlfriend Jeannine Gautreau and the many overnights at her house. We still keep in touch when I visit. She married my cousin Roger Cormier who is also one of my favorite persons.

Who could forget those memorable skating parties in the moonlight on the marshes. It would involve the entire high school students that wished to participate. We would get someone to drive us there and pick us up later. We would light up a tire to warm ourselves up and just skate the night away. We would practice doing tricks and how to skate as a couple. Everybody got along great. Due to my dad being strict, I was not allowed to date at sixteen which is quite different then now. I was allowed to go with groups like this.

Chapter 16

In 1955, Mom and Dad decided that we needed to be together again as a family. So we took out our papers and with Uncle Patrick (Dad's brother) sponsoring us we also moved to the USA. Uncle Patrick got Dad a job as janitor in the factory he worked in. There were difficult times for mom and dad. It was a big adjustment for them. First of all, living in apartments is quite different than having your own house. As luck would have it, our first apartment on Myrtle Street, Waltham Mass. was a nightmare. We lived on the second floor and the woman on the first floor would not allow any noise at all. She did not like our country music, we could not have any company, we could not walk upstairs with shoes on, especially heels, because she would take a broom handle and bang on the pipes driving us crazy. If we had company, she would call the police even in broad daylight. My mom was getting so nervous we were worrying about her. So finally the woman convinced the landlord to evict us. I was so happy when that happened that I was shouting hurrah and jumping up and down. I hated that apartment because of her. I heard through the grapevine that she got three or four families evicted before the landlord figured out it was her and told her to get out.

Our next apartment on Exchange Street, Waltham, Mass was too small for us but we took it because we were pressed for time since having to get out of the other place. I loved living there. The people were all friendly and there were French speaking people there for mom. She could finally relax and she felt better about living in the USA. Another obstacle for my parents was having to speak English. Dad picked it up faster because of working on the outside and dealing with co workers.

With Mom we all spoke French in the house so she was not practicing and she was more shy and self conscious than Dad. For the siblings, we all adjusted quickly having learned English in school. Jeannette and I went job hunting at sixteen and eighteen. Our first job was at a paper bag company. We did okay but it was a little rough for a first job. It was piece work and you had to be relieved by another person even if it was to go to the ladies room otherwise you would have paper bags all over the place. They did not stop that machine for anything. Our cousin Corrine LeBlanc was working at Clevite Transistor, a factory, so she went to her boss to try and get us a job there and she was successful. We left the Paper Bag Co. and went to work at Clevite Transistor. It was more money and better suited to us. We really liked it there and I was employed there until 1960.

Chapter 17

In 1957, I met my husband Salvatore Russo. I was at a tavern called Ma's at the time with my sister Jeannette and my cousin Eva. The owner was friends with my parents so she would let us come in and listen to the country band. She would only serve us coke and would not let any boys sit with us or bother us unless we said it was ok. On that one night, my husband who was in the Air Force and stationed at Hanscom field in Bedford, Mass. was there with his buddies. He had met my cousin Eva before and used knowing her as an excuse to come and meet me. I liked him immediately even though he had to borrow money to buy us a coke. He asked to take me home and I agreed on one condition that he take us all home. He agreed and took us home. He then made a date to take me to Revere Mass. (an amusement park). I said ok and fell in love with him on that first date. It was love at first sight. He only has one sister so meeting my family was a challenge. The first day he picked me up at work and came to dinner at my house. I thought my mom would die she was so nervous. He was the first English speaking person she really had to interact with and first boy friend that was not from Canada. My two brother-in laws are French Canadians. Secondly my mom was serving paspierre which is strictly a French Canadian meal. The closest description I can give is that it looks like a blade of grass and it is picked near the ocean. I think it would be called a sea weed in English but I do not really know. Anyway, Mom said, "he is American and he will never like paspierre and I am so embarrassed". I told mom do not worry it will be ok. Well Sal (as I call him for short) absolutely loved it and had two or three servings.

Mom and Dad liked him immediately and also for his personality because they were so at ease with him.

When I first started going out with Sal, his job in the Air Force was maintenance mechanic on the planes and he was also on the flying status. Being on the flying status meant that he would fly with the crew when they had a mission tracking down weather balloons. These balloons were for atmospheric experiments and to obtain information. At times he would be gone for quite a few days. While he was gone, his buddies were really funny. They would look after me and if a guy came around they would say she is taken. If I had wanted to cheat they would not have allowed it. He was gone on one of these missions to California right before our wedding and it was very close. We were panicking that he was not going to make it home on time. It was stressful but yet I was happy he was gone because I caught the mumps from my little brother Bert and I did not want Sal to see my fat looking cheeks.

Another funny episode that happened with those flying missions was when we were newly wed, Sal had to fly out and he was feeling bad about leaving me. So he came home to see me right after work and was told to be back by 6:00 pm. The pilot, knowing he was newly wed and not wanting to leave me decided to play a joke on him. Instead of waiting until 6:00 pm, he left at 5:00 pm without Sal. When Sal got there and found out the plane was gone, he was all scared because he had been told it was very serious to miss a flight. So when he returned home he was really upset and remained that way the whole weekend wondering what they were going to do to him. When he got back to the base, the pilot was laughing his head off and teased him.

That is how these guys were always kidding around. But it was not funny to Sal. He would give up flying status not too long after that.

Later on he met the rest of the family and dealt with the sticky lollypops and all that comes with having 6 kids at the time all around the same age between all my sisters and Bertrand. He really got a kick out of Bertrand especially when he used to act up since he was a very active boy. One night Sal was over and we were all sitting at the table eating dinner. Bertrand was messing around with his potatoes and I told him to stop. He got angry and threw his fork at me and got me in the forehead. It did not really hurt me but Sal could not believe it. He was shocked. But like I mentioned earlier, a lot of the blame was not my parents but the siblings for spoiling him. Today Bertrand is a wonderful and thoughtful person. He was only four years old then.

Sal and I got engaged at Christmas time 1957 and we had a short engagement. My folks and I lived on Exchange Street in Waltham Mass at the time. There was a funny incident that happened there with my dad that Sal still talks about to this day. One night Sal and I had a date and he was over my house. Mom kept complaining to Dad how she was cold. After a while Dad became annoyed with her complaining and went down cellar and loaded the furnace with wood. After a while it became so hot you could see the flames coming out of the floor grates and we were dying with the heat. All of a sudden the tenant upstairs comes flying out of his apartment in his underwear asking what the heck is going on. My Dad says to Mom, "I do not think you will be complaining about being cold again tonight. It was irresponsible and dangerous to do but it was also funny. My Dad was overly serious and responsible which made this episode even funnier.

Chapter 18

In the beginning of 1958 my family moved to Lawton Place, Waltham Mass. Sal, wanting to help my parents and save them some money, said he would get a truck from the motor pool at Hanscom field air force base to move us. Well, the Sergeant in charge of the motor pool at the base gave him a few lessons on how to drive the truck. In order to shift gears on the truck, you had to double clutch it. If you didn't do this, you would be grinding in the process of shifting gears. Driving from the base on highway 128 was fine. No gear shifting cruising on the highway. When he reached the city limits of Waltham, there was nothing but grinding gears all the way to Exchange Street, and to Lawton Place. We were lucky we accomplished the move without ruining the truck! But you know, being young and all he was pretty spunky at trying things. Lawton Place was a much roomier apartment and better suited to the family size, but I would forever miss Exchange Street.

Chapter 19

Sal and I got married on July 5th 1958 and went on to have three children, Carl, Debra and Gary. Sal was still in the Air Force with one more year to go. I did not mind the Air Force since it was just like having a job. We lived off the base and he was gone 7:00 am to 3:00 pm which was not different than holding down a job. He decided not to re-enlist in 1959 for personal reasons, therefore becoming a civilian again. Employment was a little tough then and getting a job was not easy but I managed to get him an interview at Clevite Transistor where I was employed and he got hired. We were working in the same place until spring of 1960 when I left to have my first child. I did not return to work. I became a housewife raising the children. Sal continued to work there until 1965 when Clevite Transistor went out of business. Sal really liked that job and missed it for a long time. He then worked at Polaroid for a while and then Adams Russell. Then we made the decision to move to Middletown, Connecticut, Sal's birth place. We moved in 1971 to 24 McKenna Drive, Middletown, CT.

Sal upon coming to Middletown worked at E.I.S. for a while then Custom Maintenance for a while. From there he worked at Jarvis Corporation from 1977 until 1998 when he retired.

Chapter 20

I was lonesome for my family for a while and decided to get involved in Brownies and Girl Scouts with my daughter Debra just to get out and be a part of something. I was involved for quite a while and was a combination Leader and Coordinator. As coordinator, I recruited new leaders and helped them get started. I was also a helper at times in Cub Scouts with my son Gary.

The two boys joined the youth hockey league at Wesleyan and Sal and I were taking the boys all over and watching the games. We really enjoyed those years. Debra was in dancing school so we also had dance recitals to attend. The boys were also in Little League baseball. It seems like a lot of rushing around while you are doing it but when it is over you miss it.

I then gave up all the volunteering and went to work part

time in Sears Roebuck making the sale signs that were throughout the store. I worked there until 1977 and then went to work full time in Safeway Products. Safeway Products was sold to B.F. Goodrich in 1994 and I continued working there until 2003 when they moved to Union West Virginia. Being close to 65 years old, I decided to retire.

Chapter 21

In 1992, I proudly became a citizen of the United States of America. It was such an honor and I now have dual citizenship. I am so happy because now I can vote and have a voice in the selection of our presidents.

Chapter 22

Jeannette is two years older than me but we were in the same grade in school. We had no teachers in the little school house for a few years so we started school the same time. We were both smart in school but I could never quite beat her because she was a little smarter. We were very different in nature and interests growing up so we were not very close. Growing older has changed that and we really enjoy each other's company now. She used to be too serious growing up but now she is open to having fun.

In 1960, Jeannette married Robert Patriquin. They would go on to have three children, Eric, Ralph and Craig.

Chapter 23

My Mom and Dad ended up with seventeen grand children. On Christmas day when all these grand children were small, we would gather at my parent's house for the big meal. Talk about a large crowd. We would have so much fun together. This is terrible but one Christmas we lost Daniel O'Brien (Laurida & Tilmon's son). He walked out the door with his new little toy gun and was just walking the streets. He must have been around four or five years old. We did not see him leave but a little while later realized he was not in the house. A bunch of us started searching the area and riding around and could not find him. Finally, we went to the police station to report it and there was Daniel sitting there eating an ice cream cone and talking to the police. The police saw this kid walking the streets and picked him up and took him to the station. We were sure glad to get him back. In my family, there were a lot of children the same age since there always seemed to be three sisters pregnant at the same time. There are a lot of years with trio children for instance my three all have matching cousins on the year they are born.

Chapter 24

1978 would turn out to be a bad year for us since we lost our dad. After suffering a massive heart attack a few years earlier he was left with angina chest pain. When his diseased gall bladder acted up a few years later it was too much for his heart and he passed away. Being our first close family loss it was hard on everybody.

Chapter 25

Now I would like to elaborate more into my children's accomplishments. They have made me very proud. Carl upon graduation from Vinal Technical Regional High School, went to work with his dad at Jarvis Corporation. There he learned to setup and make gears. He worked there for a number of years. Then he left to go work at Aero Gear in Windsor. After going to school for the company a number of times, he is presently working in the engineering department designing gears.

In 2002, our son Carl married Pamela Menard. We are very happy to have her in our family. She is an interior decorator.

Chapter 26

Debra upon graduation from Middletown High School tried college and found it was not for her. So she left and did some waitressing jobs at different restaurants and then tried banking and factory work. She was not getting anywhere so I talked her into going to CPI school for computer courses. After that she was placed in an accounting firm where she did secretarial work.

In 1987, our daughter Debra married Abel Picard. We are very fond of our son-in-law Abel. He works at Durham Manufacturing as a supervisor.

Debra got a job in Chester as an administrating secretary and set up the entire shop and inventory and did a great job. She started her family and left to stay home with her children, Austin & Nevin. We are happy that they gave us two grand children.

They are a great part of our lives and we love them dearly.

Upon returning to work part time, she worked for a construction company and next for the Town of Wethersfield in the Building Department. Then wanting full time, she applied and got a job as Administrative Assistant in the Building Department for the Town of Middlefield.

Chapter 27

Gary upon graduating from Vinal Technical High School joined the Air Force following in his Dad's footsteps. In the Air Force he went to school for water treatment plant operation and that became his job in the Air Force. He was stationed in Germany which he loved. He made a lot of good friends there. He served 4 years. When he came back home he got a job at Mattabasset treatment plant, then at East Hampton and from there the Southington Water Plant where he is presently employed for a lot of years.

Chapter 28

In 1988 we had a sad experience. Mom passed away unexpectedly because of a botched surgery. We were devastated because at 81 years old and the good health she experienced before that did not prepare us for the out come. We all felt she should have had a lot of more good years with us. But I guess destiny thought differently.

Chapter 29

In my family, it was always custom when a family member was moving, we did not hire movers. Instead, all the men in the family moved the big items. Well my sister Jeannette was moving so Sal was helping. It was a hot balmy Friday night and all of a sudden a moth flew inside Sal's ear. Well Sal was going crazy every time the moth would start to flutter in his ear. So finally, they had to take him to the emergency room. Well the Doctor on duty was trying to flush the moth out with water and was having a terrible time. After enough flushing and reaching in with tweezers, they finally got it out. Would you believe that moth was still alive? Sal had to put antibiotic drops in the ear for a while to make sure the moth did not lay eggs in his ear. It was not funny but I could not help saying it could only happen to you and laughing. Poor guy.

Chapter 30

I would like to share some beautiful memories of my mom and dad's fiftieth anniversary. Due to the fact that all mom and dad's brothers and sisters and best man and maid of honor were in Canada, my two brothers decided to hold the celebration in Canada. What a wonderful idea that was! The whole family traveled to Canada and we all stayed in the old homestead. All of the cousins had so much fun sleeping on the floor in sleeping bags and laughing and talking half the night away. They taught each other how to dance for the party and danced together at the party and had a ball. Mom and dad started the event by renewing their vows at St. Thomas Church in St. Joseph, New Brunswick, Canada. It was such a beautiful touching ceremony with their original best man and maid of honor by their side and all their children and grand children looking on. Then we had a wonderful reception in Moncton with all their brothers and sisters and friends in attendance. I know Canada appreciated us too. We were going through home made bread bought in College Bridge as fast as they could make it with the crowd that we were. That is not counting the rest of the food we were buying. They must have missed our business after we left.

Chapter 31

The worst tragedy in my life struck in January of 1997. The loss of my brother at 54 years old has been the hardest thing for me to accept. I would cry in the shower every morning for months and months. I would also cry walking to work and compose myself in time to enter work. I could not talk about it for a long time. I am ok now although at times I like to talk to him.

Dollard and I were inseparable before I met Sal. After I got married, we drifted apart somewhat but he still was always in my heart. I used to go to Dollard all the time when I could not figure something out because he was always so logical and smart. He was the family cornerstone and strength. He did a beautiful job of taking care of mom and dad also. He was the first in the family to go to college and graduated with two majors, mechanical and electrical engineering and did it on his own. I love you Dollard and may you rest in peace with God in heaven.

Chapter 32

Sal and I love to travel. We discovered that on our 25th anniversary. Our children were all old enough to leave alone since we had them so young. So we started to brainstorm about where to go for our 25th. We were talking short range trips and finally I just said, "why not dream big? How about Hawaii? Sal said, "We can't afford that financially". I said, "How do you know? Let's check it out". So we went to a travel agency and voila they had a special anniversary package that included everything we wanted at a price we could afford. So we were off to Hawaii. We were so excited. They served us champagne on the plane. Hawaii as far as I am concerned is better and more mystical than anything else I have seen. The temperature and the gorgeous rainbows after the showers is just the beginning of the beauty in Hawaii. There are flowers every where and the hotel lobbies are beautiful. From there we did California, the Carribean, The Bahamas, Mexico, Cabo San Lucas, British Columbia, cruises and others. I hope we can travel again before we leave this earth.

Chapter 33

Finally as I am coming close to closing out my life's highlights, I could not do that without adding my wonderful in-laws. I married into a wonderful, warm Sicilian Italian family that welcomed me into their family with open arms down to the cousins. I will never forget the wonderful backyard picnics given by cousin Lucy DeFrancesco along with my mother-in-law's great crab spaghetti sauce which everybody loved. We also had some great wiffle ball games and horseshoe games there. The beach parties we had were also nothing to sneeze at with all the food. To know Italians is to know good food. They are noted for that.

Thanks Phil Mariani for always being there over and beyond expectation and for the fun time going out as couples. A big thank you to all the other cousins for all your help when we first came to live in Connecticut. It has not been forgotten. Regrets would be losing my father-in-law so young. I was very fond of him and had some nice quiet conversations with him.

Chapter 34

I would now like to share our vacation at the beach in Sound View. We rented this large cottage there. There was Sal and I and our three children, Phil, Josie and son Philip, Lucy and her three children Donna, Elaine and Mark. There was enough beds for all these people and the kitchen table was big enough to accommodate fourteen people. We had such a good time and I must say it was not your typical beach living. The meals consisted of roast beef and the trimmings, veal cutlets, spaghetti and an occasional hot dog. Sal's uncle drove there with his truck loaded with all this gear which was above board but what the heck. In the morning it was a rush who would get the shower first which was located outside and only had hot water for two showers and the rest got cold. Thank God for Donna, Elaine, Philip and Mark they taught us the latest dances and baby sat our small children so we could have some nightlife fun. When the weekend rolled around, Uncle Angelo, Aunt Lula, Mom, Angela and Aunt Minnie joined us. It was so much fun to the point that I was lonesome when I went back home. It would turn out to be one of my most memorable weeks at the beach.

Chapter 35

Now as Sal and I sail into our golden years together we are enjoying each other's company as well as our time spent on our computers. We are also movie buffs going every Saturday afternoon. We love to eat out as often as possible. We love the Red Sox and watching the games on TV. We do still love to travel although personal reasons stop us right now. I love to read Mary Higgins Clark's books. I also love to do crossword puzzles, find the hidden objects and find the hidden words and the jumble puzzles in the Courant. I try to walk my five miles five days a week and I am learning line dancing in my basement. I also love to listen to my French Canadian station CJSE on Sundays from 2:00 to 6:00 USA time.

We also enjoy our grandchildren Austin and Nevin and help them whenever they need us. Sal swims five days a week at the

YMCA. Last but not least Sal and I are coming to our 50th anniversary July 5th. We have already renewed our wedding vows in April in St. Pius Church which gave us great pleasure and we are hoping that God continues to give us good health for a lot more years.

On July 5th, (our anniversary) the children gave us a beautiful golden anniversary celebration at the Elks Club in Rocky Hill. All our favorite people were there and Sal and I felt truly honored. Life has been good to us. A big thank you to Carl, Debra, Gary, Pamela, Abel, Austin and Nevin for the party.

Chapter 36

When the family first moved to the United States, we all lived close to each other in Massachusetts. Later on due to employment or family obligations, the siblings all separated. In 1971, I was the first to move to Connecticut which is my husband Sal's birth place. Lorraine and Oswald moved to Maine. Bertrand moved to New York. Mom, Dad, Dollard and Jeannette stayed in Massachusetts. We now all live in Different States with one out of the country.

Therefore, in the year 2002, I decided to initiate the first Belliveau family reunion. My reason, I felt the need to reconnect with all my nieces and nephews and to get to know their spouses and their children. It was a great success. My daughter Debra and son-in-law Abel volunteered their yard and we had campers and tents all over the yard. It was so heart warming to see everybody reconnect and catch up on where their lives are today. I learned for the first time how great a guitar player my nephew Paul O' Brien was and how the O'Brien siblings Paul, Daniel, Kenneth and Timmy could sing and harmonize as well as all the happenings in the lives of my nieces and nephews. It was also great for my children to get to know their cousins better. We have continued the family reunions. It is held every two years. We have three hosts and alternate between the Russos in Connecticut, The O'Brien's in Massachusetts and the Bourques in Maine. I hope it continues.

Chapter 37

I also would like to mention some of my e-mail buddies whom I communicate with frequently. Carol Penta (long time good friend), Jeannette (my sister), Francis Richard (my Canadian School friend), Edna Brown (former boss), Claudine (my Canadian niece), Sara Fite (second cousin). Love you guys. Keep those emails coming.

Hope you have enjoyed reading my Auto-Biography "JUST A FARM RAISED CANUCK BY ROSE ALINE (BELLIVEAU) RUSSO as much as I enjoyed writing it.